Plínio Mamprim
Mateus Terra

I.o.T - INTERNET OF THINGS IN THE LOGISTICS SUPPLY CHAIN

Plínio Mamprim
Mateus Terra

I.o.T - INTERNET OF THINGS IN THE LOGISTICS SUPPLY CHAIN

The effective improvement and the real gain in the implementation of the I.o.T and its tools in the logistic system.

ScienciaScripts

Imprint
Any brand names and product names mentioned in this book are subject to trademark, brand or patent protection and are trademarks or registered trademarks of their respective holders. The use of brand names, product names, common names, trade names, product descriptions etc. even without a particular marking in this work is in no way to be construed to mean that such names may be regarded as unrestricted in respect of trademark and brand protection legislation and could thus be used by anyone.

Cover image: www.ingimage.com

This book is a translation from the original published under ISBN 978-620-2-56034-4.

Publisher:
Sciencia Scripts
is a trademark of
International Book Market Service Ltd., member of OmniScriptum Publishing Group
17 Meldrum Street, Beau Bassin 71504, Mauritius
Printed at: see last page
ISBN: 978-620-2-69410-0

SUMMARY

1. INTRODUCTION

Aiming and always seeking to improve the functioning of the logistics supply chain management, this book, based on the most current literature on the I.o. theme. T, comes to provide knowledge about the Internet of Things in the logistic supply chain, involving bibliographic research in its total part, always focused on cost reductions, both for entrepreneurs and final consumers, through solutions in the field of logistics.

When we talk about logistics we have a simplistic view of this area of knowledge, of its great importance in all the management of a company, or even in our lives, of how influential it is in our society (world), of the benefits for the final consumers, when we have an efficient planning of logistics in the company.

Daskin (1995) defines logistics as the planning and operation of physical systems (vehicles, warehouses, transportation networks, etc.), informational and managerial systems (data processing, teleinformatics, managerial control processes, etc.).) necessary for inputs and products to economically overcome physical and temporal conditions.

Linked to logistics, we have the Supply Chain, which in turn plays a key role in organizational logistics management. Doing all the planning of purchasing inputs, storage, until the delivery of this product to its final consumer.

Supply chains are networks of organizations responsible for the different processes and activities that produce value in the form of products and services made available to the end consumer. Supply chain management is concerned with external flows to the company and aims to coordinate and control materials, information and finances that go from the supplier to the consumer, including manufacturers, wholesalers and retailers (Ballou, 2006).

With the advancement of global technology and improvements in the distribution of the Internet to the world, we have achieved amazing developments in every imaginable area. One of them is the I.o.T (Internet of Things), which with its vast area of applications promises unimaginable benefits.

Along the way this study has been carried out, its first mention is cited by Kevin Ashton, co-founder of the *Massachusetts Institute of Technology* (MIT) *Auto-ID Center,* in his article in 1999. Kevin writes "cyber-physical systems (CPS) is the thread that connects the entire industrial Internet of things. It is the indispensable technological link for the fusion between the real and virtual worlds".

For full operation we have to acquire the tools, with these tools we can seek the gains and cost reductions, more than expected. Some of these tools are: RFID, GPS, ERP, DRONE and NFC that are connected to each other, to successfully carry out all this system, providing the satisfaction of all the beneficiaries of the companies that use this means.

1.1.   WORK GOALS

1.1.1.   OVERALL PURPOSE

The objective of this study is to show the effective improvement and the real gain in the implementation of I.o.T and its tools in the logistic system.

1.1.2.   SPECIFIC OBJECTIVE

The specific objective of this book is to carry out surveys and analyses based on bibliographic research, encouraged by an *in loco* experience, on the implementation of the internet of things (I.o.T) in the logistics supply chain of companies, to show the benefits of this technology in favor of logistics development.

2. METHODOLOGY

The methodology used for the survey and basis of this work is based on the studies through the Bibliographical Review and study of recent cases on the subject. According to GIL (2010), the Bibliographical Review is a survey based on material already published and this modality includes, among others, printed material, books, magazines, newspapers, theses, dissertations. Also according to the author, due to the dissemination of new information formats, this research may include other types of sources, such as websites and electronic journals.

3. BIBLIOGRAPHICAL REVIEW

3.1. LOGISTICS

For Ballou (2006), logistics deals with all handling and storage activities, which facilitate the flow of products from the point of raw material acquisition to the point of final consumption, as well as the information flows that set the products in motion, with the purpose of providing adequate service levels to customers at a reasonable cost.

Daskin (1995) defines logistics as the planning and operation of physical (vehicles, warehouses, transportation networks, etc.), informational and managerial systems (data processing, teleinformatics, management control processes, etc.) necessary for inputs and products to economically overcome physical and temporal constraints.

For Novaes (1989), logistics is the science that aims to solve problems of supply of inputs to the productive sector (sources of supply, storage policies, means of transportation used, etc.), problems of distribution of finished and semi-finished products (storage, order processing, transfer, distribution, etc.) and other general logistics problems such as location of warehouse facilities, information processing, etc. All this seeking to encompass both spatial constraints (moving products from production points to consumption centers) and temporal constraints (requiring strict delivery times, operational reliability levels, etc.).

Christopher (1997) adopts a concept very similar to the one presented above and suggests that the main concept of logistics is the process of strategically managing the acquisition, movement and storage of materials, parts and finished products throughout the organization in order to maximize present and future profitability by meeting orders at low costs. This author states that the scope of logistics extends throughout the organization, from the management of raw materials to the delivery of the final product.

3.2 SUPPLY CHAIN

Supply chain is the group of suppliers that supplies the needs of a company in the creation and development of its products. It can also be understood as a form of collaboration between suppliers and consumers for the creation of value.

Also, supply chain can be defined as the life cycle of processes comprising the physical, informational, financial and knowledge flows, the objective of which is to satisfy the requirements of the final consumer with products and services from several connected suppliers. The supply chain, however, is not limited to the flow of products or information in the sense of Customer Vendor. There is also a flow of information, complaints and products, among others, in the sense of Customer Supplier (AYERS, 2001).

According to Ballou (2006) supply chain is a set of functional activities (transportation, stock control, etc.) that are repeated countless times along the channel through which raw materials are being converted into finished products, to which value is added to the consumer.

For Christopher (1998), it is a network of organizations that are involved through *downstream* and *upstream* links in the different processes and activities that produce value in the form of products and services released to the end consumer. Lambert *et al.* (1998), however, defines the supply chain as not just a one-to-one business chain, but a network of multiple businesses and relationships. Mentzer *et al.* (2001) defines it as the set of three or more organizations directly involved in the upstream or downstream flows of products, services, financial and information from the primary source to the final customer.

3.3 INTERNET OF THINGS (I.o.T)

The term *Internet of Things* was coined in 1999 by Kevin Ashton, co-founder of the *Auto-ID Center at the Massachusetts Institute of Technology* (MIT). In a recent article,(Ashton, 2009), he stated that the original idea of IoT foresaw the connection of all physical objects to the Internet, with the ability to capture information through radio frequency identification (RFID) and sensing technologies - which would allow them to observe, identify and understand the world regardless of people and their limitations of time, attention and accuracy. In 2005 the International Telecommunication Union (ITU) predicted that the possibility of unique item identification, coupled with sensor technologies and the ability to interact with the environment would create an Internet of things (ITU, 2012).

In a didactic approach, it defines four stages of Internet evolution: Web 1.0, focused on connecting and obtaining information on the Net; Web 2.0 or Social Web, characterized by concern with the user experience and collaboration through social networks; Web 3.0 or Semantic Web, with efforts focused on assigning meaning and context to information; and the current stage, the Ubiquitous Web, constituted by the Internet of Things, based on connectivity and interactivity between people, information, processes and objects, through technologies that allow access to the network by anyone, from anywhere, at any time, using any device, including multifunctional equipment with intelligent sensors, such as appliances, cars, clothes, etc., from applications that dynamically adapt to the needs of users (DAVIS, 2008)

The I.o. T describes a system in which the elements in the physical world, and sensors inside or attached to those elements, are connected to the Internet through wireless and wired Internet connections. In his article, Ashton wrote:

> "If we had computers that knew everything about things in general -- using data they collected without our help -- we'd be able to track and tell everything, and greatly reduce waste, loss, and costs. We'd know when to replace, repair, or recall a product, and whether it's new or outdated. We need to empower computers with their own means of collecting information, so they can see, hear, and smell the world on their own, with all their random glory. RFID and sensor technology enable computers to observe, identify and understand the world without the limitations of data entered by humans". (Ashton, 1999).

Technological advances in recent years have made it possible for the Internet of Things not only to be attached to RFID, but to connect the whole world in real time, providing almost infinite improvements in all existing media.

The simplest way of thinking about I.o. T is to consider it as the network Connection of physical objects. With the advent of I.o.T, Internet connections now extend to objects that are not computers in the classical sense, and in fact serve a multitude of other purposes. A shoe, for example, is intended to cushion the foot while walking or running. A street light illuminates a road or sidewalk. A forklift is used to move pallets or other heavy items. None of them have traditionally been connected to the Internet, they did not send, receive, process or store information.

However, there is latent information on all these items and their use. When we connect, when we light "dark assets" large amounts of emerging information along with potential new insights and business value.

A connected shoe can tell its owner (or a researcher, or a manufacturer) the number of steps in a given period of time, or force with which the foot hits the ground.

A connected street, the light can feel the presence of cars and provide information for drivers or city officials to plan routes and optimize traffic flow. A connected forklift can alert a manager to an imminent mechanical problem or safety risk, or be used to create greater warehouse location intelligence.

The I. o. T is in the disconnected connection, it's just part of the story. Along with physical objects, people and intangible goods "things" must also be connected in new and better ways.

I. o. T is a vital facilitator of certain types of connection that together, the networking of physical objects, but also includes the links between people, processes and data definitions of I. o. T settings are almost as diverse as their applications. However, most observers agree that I.o. T implies value beyond the physical or logical interconnection of objects.

The I. o. T is becoming more important and popular every day because, according to Dias (2016) everything can be connected at low cost and high speed, each I. o. equipment. T has a unique identity, information processing is becoming cheaper and cheaper, the evolution of sensors - cheaper and miniaturized - allow different applications and information storage in the cloud is more available and data analysis algorithms are faster every day.

In this sense, the author stresses that:

> In view of the growing popularity of IoT, there is no single concept destined for this system. Experts have different interpretations of this concept and each organization describes the IoT system according to its preference or market vision (DIAS, 2016, p. 19).

The CASAGRAS project (*Coordination and Support Action for Global RFID - related Activities and Standardisation*) brings a definition to the I. o system. T system, and was translated by Professor José Roberto de Almeida Amazonas *apud* Dias (2016), where:

> [...] a global network infrastructure, interconnecting physical and virtual objects through the exploration of data capture and communication capabilities. This infrastructure includes the existing and evolving Internet as well as network

developments. It will offer specific object identification, sensing and connection capabilities as the basis for the development of independent cooperative applications and services. These will be characterized by a high degree of autonomous data capture, event transfer, connectivity and network interoperability (DIAS, 2016, p. 20).

Today, the objects around everyone are becoming more and more intelligent due to technological innovations and various industries are being impacted. The I.o. T, the new technological paradigm, is conquering the entire world, connecting virtually everything around us, from the simplest to the most sophisticated objects.

3.4 TOOLS FOR THE USE OF I. O. T IN THE LOGISTICS CHAIN

In order for this whole Internet of Things system to function properly, you need the tools that make up this system. Those being the tools: RFID, GPS, ERP, DRONE, NFC and I.A. that are connected to each other, to successfully make this whole system. So we have to evaluate the Cyberphysical System, which is the wire that connects all the industrial Internet of things. It is the technological link that is indispensable for the fusion between the real and virtual worlds, it is the one that makes all the junction between I.o.T and its tools, the link of extreme importance for the total operation, of the successful management foreseen with the implementation of this system.

3.4.1 CYBERPHYSICAL SYSTEM

The Cyberphysical system can be understood as the link between the Real World and Cyberspace or even the thread that unites the whole I. o. T. Cyberphysical Systems (CPS) is considered the technological link indispensable for the fusion between the real and virtual worlds.

CPS are used wherever complex physical systems need to communicate with the digital world to enable their performance to be optimized and their efficiency improved. They play an increasing role in the industrial process and production control (intelligent plant), particularly in the context of I.o.T. CPS are also used in today's power supply, traffic control and driver assistance, as well as in many other areas.

Cyberphysical systems consist of objects with integrated *software* and electronics that are connected to each other or via the Internet to form a single networked system. It includes sensors and components to move or control a mechanism or system, the so-called actuators, so that it can connect the CPS to the outside world. The sensors allow the system to acquire and process the data.

The data is then made available to network-based services that use actuators to directly impact measurements taken in the real world. This leads to the merging of the physical and cyberspace worlds within the Internet of Things.

Cyber-physical systems are used in industrial production to build Internet-based architectures that facilitate the remote control of *stand-alone* production systems. CPS are valuable tools in many other application fields: integrated into an intelligent network, they can control a power grid of tomorrow or control traffic to make it safer and reduce carbon dioxide emissions.

In the following figure 01, we can see the connection of the Industry with its means of operation, through the use of the I.oT with the cyberphysical system.

Figure 1 Total interaction with I.o.T.

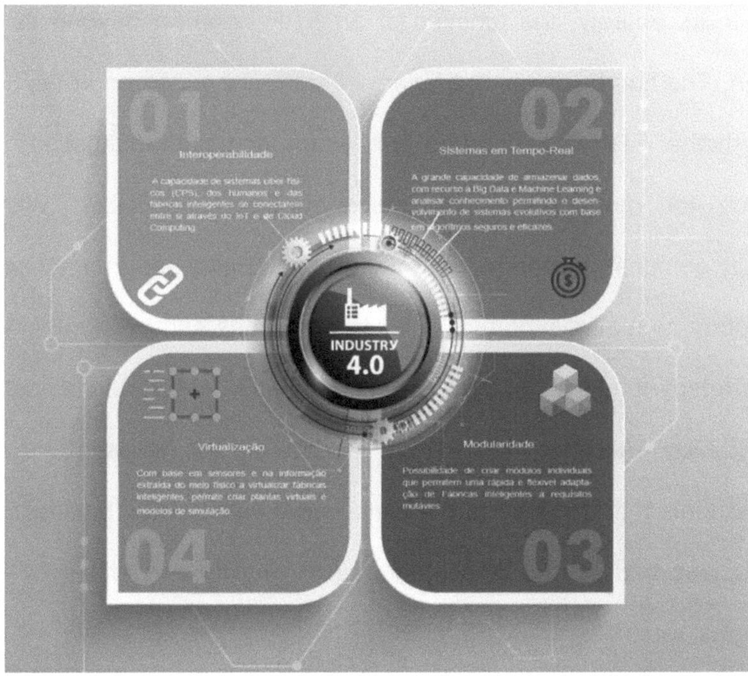

Source: Invoke, *online*, 2017.

3.4.2 ERP - Enterprise *Resource Planning* or Enterprise Management System.

Exemplifying in an efficient way what is an ERP - an acronym for *Enterprise Resource Planning*, or Enterprise Management System - one could say that it is a corporate software that has as main function to support companies in the total control of their information, integrating and managing data, resources and processes so that the companies have more power of decision making and success in business (Mega Sistemas, *online*, 2017).

But in its entirety, the function of an ERP goes far beyond its basic description. The first business management systems appeared in the 1950s, but the arrival of ERP happened, in fact, when increased competition made the search for more efficient planning methods inevitable. With the increasingly competitive market, one of the main challenges of any company is, even today, to maintain control of all its processes and information to find the best strategy to stand out among the competition with reduced costs and high profitability. And for this to be possible, it is necessary to have specialized tools that are able to measure every detail of the business in an automated way and in real time, guaranteeing agility and efficiency to the organizational routines.

With the characteristic of being a modular technology, that is, a set of tools that, when integrated, generate unique information for all sectors, ERP simplifies operational processes and adds intelligence, security and quality to the information, maintaining the flexibility in departmental management for each need mapped in a company.

In figure 2 below, you can see the ERP integration with the company.

Figure 2 ERP integration, in the company.

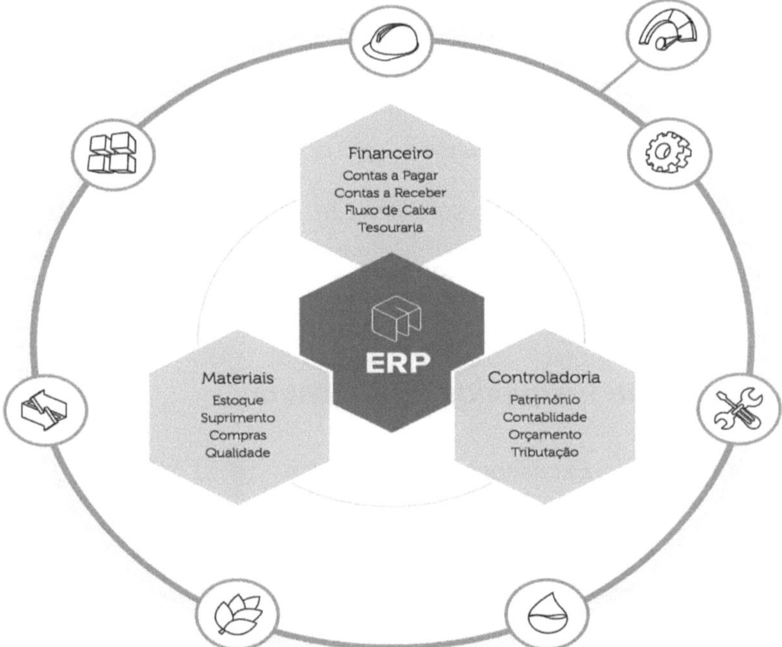

Source: Mega Sistemas, *online*, 2016.

3.4.3 GPS - Global Positioning System

The Global Positioning System (GPS) is a navigation system based on satellite signals, composed of a network of 24 satellites, placed in orbit by the U.S. Department of Defense. The GPS works in any weather condition, anywhere in the world, 24 hours a day and without any charge for the use of its signal. Initially designed for military purposes, the system soon became available for civil use in aviation, maritime surveys and for the general outdoor recreation market (GOMES, 2010).

Following the author's studies above, the basic foundations of GPS are based on determining the distance between a point, the receiver, and other reference points, the satellites. Knowing the distance that separates 3 points, it is possible to determine the position relative to those same 3 points through the intersection of 3 circles whose radius are the measured distances between the receiver and the satellites. In fact, at least 4 satellites are needed to determine our position correctly.

3.4.4 RFID -Radio *Frequency Identification*

RFID *Center Excellence* defines the RFID (*Radio Frequency Identification*) system as a technology used to identify, track and manage products and documents to animals or even individuals, without contact and without the need of a visual field. A major intensification in the use of RFID technology in logistics and retail applications is expected in the coming years, especially those focused on the supply chain. The possibility of being applied to countless situations has made RFID technology the object of several pilot projects, in different places in the world.

Composed by *transponders* (*RFtags*), readers with antennas and computer or other type of controller, RFID is an identification technology that uses radiofrequency to capture data, allowing a *tag to* be read without the need of visual field, through barriers and objects such as wood, plastic, paper, etc. A digital RFID system works as a powerful real-time data acquisition system, with the advantage of eliminating manual and visual human interventions, thus streamlining transition time and ensuring efficiency and effectiveness.

Aligning all the information from RFID *Center of Excellence*, for presenting a high degree of dynamism in the information acquisition process, without imposing great barriers to data entry, RFID is a great opportunity for Brazil in this market, especially in applications aimed at meeting specific needs of the manufacturing process of Brazilian industries.

RFID can also be used in manufacturing, logistics and distribution, providing more visibility, tracking and synchronization of the supply chain, with total reliability.

Processes such as the inventory in the distribution center, inventory or in the gondolas themselves can be done instantaneously, without errors and in real time, streamlining the operation, reducing costs, physical and accounting differences.

In addition, because it does not require manual contact, the employees will be focused on activities that add more value, directly implying in the improvement of the level of service and customer care. Below, figure 3, illustrates how RFID works.

Figure 3 - RFID operation

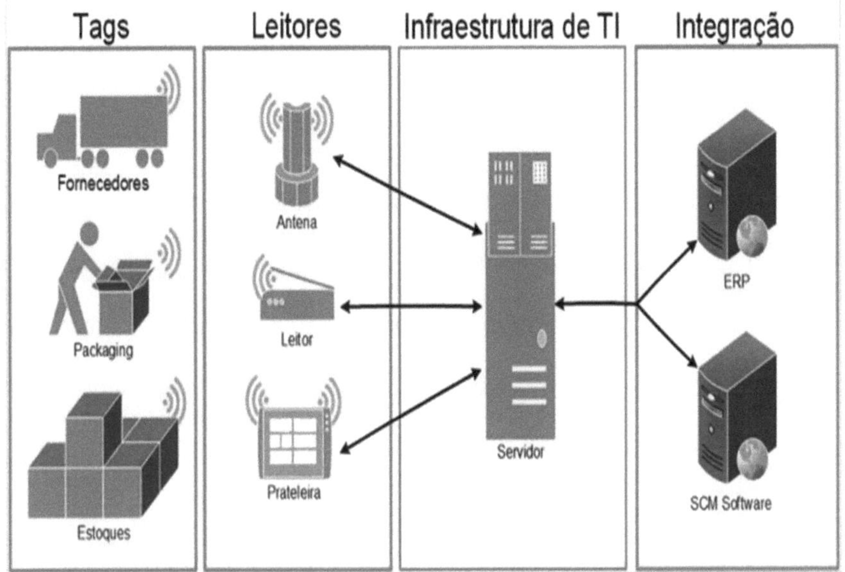

Source: Espacios magazine, *online*, 2016.

3.4.5 NFC - *NEAR FIELD COMMUNICATION*

NFC - *Near Field Communication* - is a technology that allows the exchange of information between devices without the need for cables or wires (wireless), requiring only a physical approach.

At first, NFC can be viewed merely as a wireless communication technology. But faced with so many options for this purpose, such as *Wi-Fi and Bluetooth*, what are the advantages of its adoption? The answer lies not only in what the technology is capable of doing, but mainly in how.

In short, NFC is a specification that allows *wireless* communication between two devices by simply approaching them, without the user having to type passwords, click buttons or perform any similar action when establishing the connection. Hence the name: *Near Field Communication* or Near Field Communication.

This means that as soon as the devices involved are close enough, communication is established automatically and triggers the corresponding action. These devices can be mobile phones, tablets, badges, electronic ticket cards and any other item capable of supporting the installation of an NFC chip (Infowester, *online*,2016).

3.4.3 DRONES

Drone is an English word that means "drone" in the literal translation to the Portuguese language. However, this term has become popular worldwide to designate any type of aircraft that is not manned, but commanded by human beings at a distance.

In the Portuguese language, the drones can also be called UAV ("Unmanned Aerial Vehicle") or VARP ("Remotely Piloted Air Vehicle"), acronyms that were created from the English Unmanned Aerial Vehicle - UAV.

Originally, the *drones* were designed with military objectives, to act in environments or in situations of extreme danger to humans, such as aerial combat, reconnaissance in enemy territory or searches in places contaminated with toxic substances that would be lethal to humans.

Drones, in practice, are equipment that uses a similar technology to the classic remote control vehicles. They are produced with resistant materials and remotely controlled through satellite or radio signals.

The popularity of the equipment grew at the end of the first decade of the 21st century, when *drones* began to be widely used by civilians for entertainment purposes. Photographers and cameramen, for example, use *drones* with a camera attached to them to make images from aerial angles.

For military forces, the use of *drones,* besides being more efficient, becomes much cheaper (Canaltech, *online*,2017).

3.5 I.o.T IN THE LOGISTIC SUPPLY CHAIN AND ITS BENEFITS

The supply chain comes in a great evolution and development, making possible its capacity of improvement in its processes, reducing waste of raw material, idle time, *set-ups.*

Today I.o.T comes with full force so that everything is produced, transported, at the right moments, reducing costs and expenses in an efficient and impacting way in the economy, generating an excellent revenue for the industry.

With the need to always achieve the optimal value of their processes, the industries will have in its logistic configuration a high technological development, adding a high knowledge about their customers, thus being able to have a future project on the needs and wants of their customers, a step ahead, turning the economy in an immeasurable way today, anticipating trends.

The most pleasant moment of an online purchase is the moment of delivery of such product. Imagine knowing exactly in real time where it is? Because today it is already possible through tracking, but still not in real time, now imagine knowing at the exact time that the raw material of your product has entered the manufacturing process and that it is within the quality standards of the company, that it is ready and being forwarded to you. I.o.T will provide much more than that.

And the owner of a large industry, full of projects, innovations and trends for its market, know that will always be ahead, provided high development, knowing in real time everything that came in raw material, what was produced what was sent, where, the exact moments to be done that maintenance on the equipment and what will need to be changed, without that "I think it is missing grease, but actually does not know what it is," that time will be 100% used and managed spectacularly.

No more "I think we have in stock", everything will be sure of what we have and don't have, generating order lists based on demand calculated at the exact time and period. Transforming the "not tangible" into something totally tangible and that will drive all the form of work.

Have the exact control of the activities of its employees, identifying design errors in the distribution of equipment, thus generating an environment with better quality of work satisfaction of its employees.

It is possible to see consumption information flowing directly from products to drones and autonomous vehicles, storage robots and 3D printers. Routes calculated accurately from other products in transit. Replenishment of stocks based on actual consumption, no longer on forecasts, operational problems, breaks and the need for informed maintenance directly by equipment and vehicles. Prices automatically adjusted for demand and available capacity informed by available resources and products.

The I. o. T promises far-reaching gains for operators, their business customers and end consumers. These benefits across the entire logistics value chain, including warehousing, freight and last mile delivery. And key impact areas such as operational efficiency, safety and customer demand and new business models.

With I.oT you can start to face difficult operational and business issues, bright new ways. You can automate business processes to eliminate manual interventions, improve quality and predictability, and reduce costs. You can optimize the process with people, systems and assets working together and coordinating their activities.

And, ultimately, analyses can be applied to the entire value chain to identify opportunities for improvement in practice. In essence, I. o. T in the logistics world will be about "detecting and making sense", "Detecting" is the monitoring of different assets within a supply chain through different technologies; "Making sense" is about handling sets of data that are generated as a result and then turning that data into insights that drive new solutions. (DHL and CISCO,2015).

3.6 **FINANCIAL IMPACTS**

Application of I. o. T to logistics operations promises a substantial impact. You can monitor the status of assets, parcels and people in real time throughout the value chain. You can measure the performance of these assets and make changes, what they are currently doing (and what they will do next). An analysis conducted by Cisco (the world's leading IT and networking company, being the largest information technology company in the world) in dozens of I.o. use cases. T, both in the private sector. Each use case represents a business capacity which results from the connection of the "Disconnected".

In an interview DHL (Dalsey, Hillblomand Lynn), the world's leading provider of logistics services, and Cisco, reveal figures on the impact of I.o.T on the logistics chain.

According to Cisco's economic analysis, the Internet ofThings (I.o.T), will generate an amount of $8 trillion worldwide in moving value over the next decade. This figure will come from five key drivers: innovation and revenue ($2.1 trillion); asset utilization ($2.1 trillion); supply chain and logistics ($1.9 trillion); improved employee productivity ($1.2 trillion); and more advanced customer and citizen experience ($700 billion). Figure 4 below illustrates the information above.

Figure 4 - Financial impact of I.o.T.

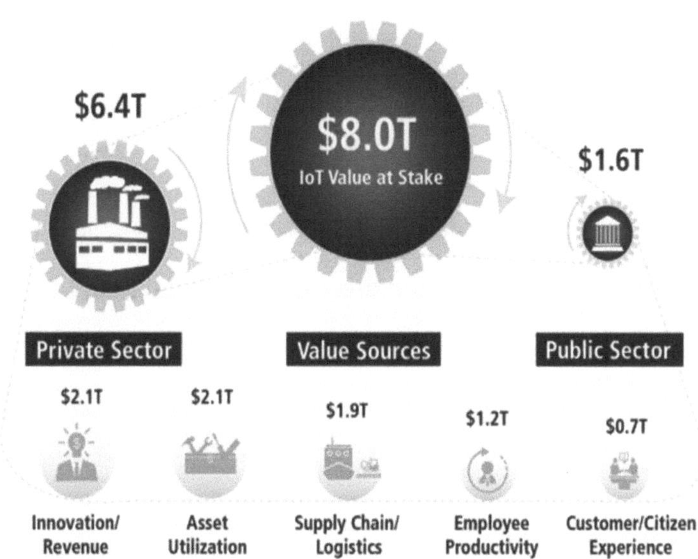

Source:DHL and CISCO, 2015.

3.7 SUCCESS CASES

3.7.1 CASE METALÚRGICA GERDAU

Through the studies carried out, it was possible to survey cases of companies that actually implemented I.o.T in their logistics chain. Three of these cases will be highlighted below, thus proving the real functionality of this technology.

As the first case, Gerdau (METALÚRGICA GERDAU S&A) won the award for best RFID (Radio Frequency Identification) case for Logistics/Supply Chain at its Ouro Branco (state of Minas Gerais) unit for structural profile products. The international award took place on May 11, 2017, in Arizona (USA), and recognizes the main case studies and best practices on supplier solutions related to Radio Frequency Identification (RFID) and Internet of Things (I. o. T) technologies of companies around the world.

Gerdau's project was born with the challenge of the logistics area to find solutions that would optimize the management of stocks and truck loads at the mill. Before arriving at Gerdau, the driver would go to the ordinance, register, wait for their release and receive a card that allowed them to enter. Inside the plant, when passing through the scale, the truck driver was directed to the loading area for structural profiles. In the sequence, he would proceed to the loading of the product, where his vehicle would wait until an employee of the Company would release the load, which was identified manually in the stock.

In the study presented, the implementation of RFID created an automatic traceability environment for the movement of products and equipment, focusing on the automation of the processes of receiving, stock management and loading. Several RFID sensors and readers were installed in the plant's internal handling equipment, such as cranes and forklifts. The process helps the employee to coordinate the loading system of the trucks in an automatic way, directing where the materials that remain in stock will be collected.

According to the industrial director of the Ouro Branco Mill, Carlos Hamilton, the company is very happy with the achievement. "At Gerdau, we do not measure our efforts when we talk about innovation and digitalization in the steel industry. In line with one of the company's main values, the initiative ensures the improvement of equipment and inventory management, guaranteeing a productivity gain in logistical operations, and also contributing to our customers' real-time tracking of their merchandise, from the plant's exit to its final destination". (Mundo Logística magazine, *online*, 2017).

3.7.2 LIVING CASE

TelefÃ³nica Brasil, through its commercial brand Vivo, expands its field of action in the Internet of Things segment.

Vivo expanded its scope of operation in the Internet of Things segment and inaugurated an innovation lab (Open I.o. T Lab) focused on developing applications with Internet of Things technology (NB-I. o. T). Based on characteristics of low power consumption, better coverage and the possibility of connecting a large number of objects, the NB-I. o. technology. T technology is the next important trend for the communications industry and is at the heart of the company's business strategy, especially in the B2B segment. The implementation of Open I. o. T Lab has the partnership and support of Huawei.

The Open I. o. T Lab, located in Rio de Janeiro, has as its main objective to drive and ensure a broad ecosystem of partners to offer the market the best commercial solutions in I. o. T and contribute to the creation of a local market in the country. These partners will also have early access to new services and solutions by combining Huawei's resources and capabilities with the resources and expertise of Vivo's Research and Development Center - where Open I. o. will be installed. T Lab - and will have several partners, such as Ublox and Quectel - that develop connectivity modules - and C.A.S Tecnologia - that develops solutions in the energy market, besides other partners.

"Internet of Things is at the core of Vivo's business strategy, which already has the leadership in the M2M market with almost 40% market share. Our goal is to complement the B2B portfolio with I. o solutions. T solutions with connectivity services, Big Data and new platforms. The partnership with Huawei will accelerate the development of these new applications and stimulate industrial synergies with other partners, anticipating and adding more functionality and intelligence in the conception of new solutions and services", explains the vice-president of B2B at Vivo, Alex Salgado.

The agreement represents a step forward for the evolution of mobile networks towards the I. o. T - a growing market, which is expected to reach almost 15 billion connections by 2020, according to Machina Research projections. Vivo already operates in traditional markets, such as means of payment, tracking and security, and also in new fronts, such as *utilities,* smart cities, *vending machines,* connected cars, measurement of TV audience, electronic billboards and even shared car. (Telefonica, *online*, 2017)

3.7.3 CASE ABINC

With the advance of i.o.t in the world, Brazil has created an association aimed at the end of the development of this technology in our country.

ABINC (Associação Brasileira de Internet das Coisas) was founded in December 2015 as a non-profit organization, by executives and entrepreneurs in the IT and Telecom market.

The idea was born from the need to create an entity that would be legitimate and representative, of national scope, and that would allow us to act in all the fronts of the Internet of Things sector.

Its objective is to encourage the exchange of information and foster commercial activity among associates; promote research and development activity; act with the government authorities involved in the Internet of Things and represent and make international partnerships with entities in the sector.

The reason for creating an Association dedicated to the Internet of Things is due to the breadth of the theme. Internet of Things is not the name of a technology, but an umbrella term that covers different technologies and verticals with profound implications for business, culture and life in society in general.

In terms of technology we can highlight the different types of devices and sensors, which have the potential to create a large electro-electronics industry in Brazil, telecommunications networks (including the new IOT data transmission networks - LPWANs - which are expanding rapidly around the world), software running on cloud servers, Applications, Big Data, Analytics and Artificial Intelligence.

And there is no industry that will remain on the fringes of the changes provided by the Internet of Things. All business verticals already have cases of IOT use with emphasis on Retail, Health, Transport and Logistics, Energy, Manufacturing (with the so-called Industry 4.0), Agribusiness, Insurance and Smart Cities. The Internet of Things will provide efficiency gains and cost reduction in the home of Trillions of dollars. But the main factor of economic importance will be the new Business Models (which currently only exist in the digital world of the Internet), but which will bring incremental revenue to all business verticals in the physical world.

And for Brazil to quickly position itself as a major world player in the Internet of Things, the formation of a strong and robust Ecosystem is a prime condition. For this, an Entity that agglutinizes and represents, in an agnostic way, all participants in this sector, large and small companies (including Start-ups), since cooperation is a vital condition for success in the Internet of Things.

4. ANALYSIS OF RESULTS

Evaluating all the research carried out in this work we identified more than significant and impacting results with the development of I.o.T in the logistic supply chain.

Seeking to better understand the benefits of all the tools that help the perfect management of I.o.T and thus making a survey of the results in values (Dollars), we obtained a chart about the I.o.T tools and their characteristics and a graph, showing the positive impact of this technology in the logistics supply chain.

Below we can see table 1 indicating the benefits of the tools mentioned.

Table 1: T.I. tools and their benefits

Tools	Benefits
RFID	-Elimination of storage errors; -Not need eye contact to read; -Easy reading in difficult-to-reach places: high, tight, dark, cold, etc; -Data storage and recording capacity.
ERP	-Process automation and manual controls; - Control over company operations; - Reduction of costs and risks; - Optimization of information flow; - Fraud reduction.
GPS	- Improved security; - Reduce operating costs; - Increase Productivity.
NFC	- Real-time or online transmission from NFC; - Significant reduction in paper expenditures; - Use of New Mobility Technologies; - Integration of physical and virtual

	sales platforms.
DRONE	- Economy in product delivery; - Agility in delivery to major cities.

Source: Survey data

Observing the values of the gains with the implementation of I.oT, based on the studies carried out by DHL and Cisco, one notices a great potential of profitability with the implementation of this technology. The analysis of chart 1 below provides an illustrative view, for better understanding. The values presented below are represented in Trillions of Dollars.

Graph 1: Profitability with the implementation of the technology

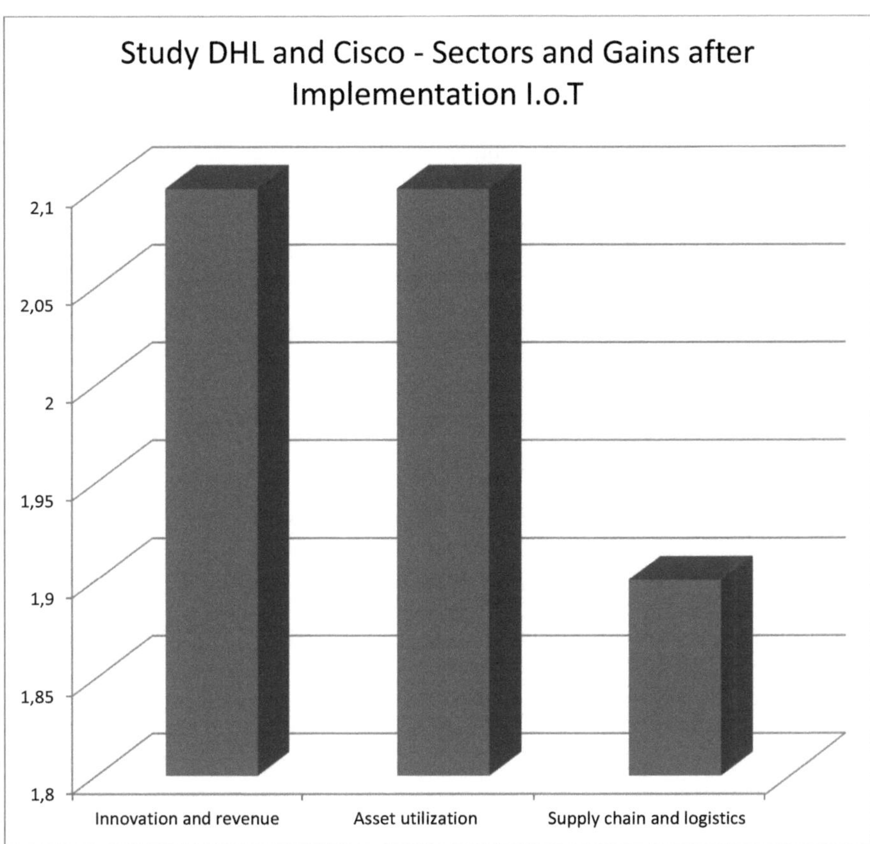

Source:DHL and CISCO, 2015.

5. FINAL CONSIDERATIONS

Winning in a market as competitive as the current scenario, possibilities are restricted, ideas are scarce, opportunities appear less frequently. The wise man is the one who sees the future and holds it by the hands always walking ahead of the competitors, but side by side with innovation and continuous steps.

In a dispersed reasoning, making your mind float in immeasurable imaginations, in intangible technologies, discrediting reality, where everything can be controlled, always seeking the unimaginable. It was with these ideas of a better future and full of innovations that today this thought that floats in technologies, is more than within our world, showing that everything is connected and managed with perfection, with the I.o.T. in the center of control.

When we think about improving and leveraging a company, we soon imagine higher productivity and faster production. But what about waste? I.o.T. more than explains, the success for such a business dream is to stop losing, to value everything that was produced, all the inputs so that everything works without waste or exaggeration, providing the greatest satisfaction of entrepreneurs and their customers, bringing the success so desired.

I.o.T has gone from a dream to become the largest virtual manager acting in the real world, in a unique way, applying its benefits and showing that it is totally viable and indispensable for a conscious and successful future.

This work fosters the search for innovation, and not for here, that this work be more than a base, but a foundation for future research in search of knowledge.

REFERENCES

ABINC (Brazilian Association of Internet of Things). Available at: < http://abinc.org.br/www/abinc/> Access on: 20 June. 2017.

ASHTON, K. That "Internet of Things" Thing.RFID Journal, 22 jun. 2009. Disponível em: <http://www.rfidjournal.com/articles/view?4986>. Acesso em: 21 fev. 2017.

Ballou, R. (2006). Supply chain management (5. ed.). Porto Alegre: Bookman.

Bowersox, D. J., Closs, D. J., & Cooper, M. B. (2006). Supply chain logistics management. Porto Alegre: Bookman

DAVIS, M. Semantic wave 2008 report: industry roadmap to Web 3.0 & Multibillion Dollar Market Opportunities. Executive Summary, 2008.

DHL Trend Report Internet of Things; DHL e CISCO, 2015.

DAYS, Renata Rampim de Freitas. Internet of things without mysteries: a new intelligence for business.1 ed. São Paulo: Netpress Books, 2016.

INFOWESTER. What is NFC (Near Field Communication)? Available at: < https://www.infowester.com/nfc.php.> Accessed on: 10 May. 2017.

LUCAS, P.; BALLAY, J.; McMANUS, M. Trillions thriving in the emerging information ecology. Hoboken, N.J: Wiley, 2012.

MEGA.What is ERP? Available at: < https://www.mega.com.br/erp/?gclid=CL_n2fX_3dMCFUsGkQod8JsN_g.> Access on: 10 May. 2017.

LOGISTICAL PANEL. Internet of things will boost the logistics sector. Available at: < http://www.painellogistico.com.br/internet-das-coisas-impulsionara-o-setor-de-logistica/.> Access on: 10 May. 2017.

MUNDO LOGISTÍCA MAGAZINE. Gerdau wins award for best rfid case for logistics. Available at: http://www.revistamundologistica.com.br/noticias/gerdau-ganha-premio-por-melhor-case-de-rfid-para-logistica.> Accessed on: 20 Feb. 2017.

SCIELO. The formation in time and space of the Internet of things. Available at: < http://www.scielo.br/scielo.php?script=sci_arttext&pid=S0101-73302016000300757&lang=pt. > . Access on: 08 Mar. 2017.

TELECOMMUNICATION STANDARDIZATION SECTOR (ITU-T). ITU-T Y.2060: Overview of the internet of things. . [S.l: s.n.]. Disponível em: <http://www.itu.int/ITU-T/recommendations/rec.aspx?rec=11559>. Acesso em: 20 fev. 2017.

TELEPHONICS. Telefonica Brasil opens IoT laboratory to develop new applications. Available at: < http://www.telefonica.com.br/servlet/Satellite?c=Noticia&cid=1386095931148&pagename=InstitucionalVivo%2FNoticia%2FLayoutNoticia01.> Access on: 20 Jun. 2017.

Printed by Books on Demand GmbH, Norderstedt / Germany